This book belongs to

....

Copyright © 2014

make believe ideas ltd

The Wilderness, Berkhamsted, Hertfordshire, HP4 2AZ, UK.
501 Nelson Place, P.O. Box 141000, Nashville, TN 37214-1000, USA.

www.makebelieveideas.com

Illustrated by Dawn Machell.
Designed by Jane Horne.

First
WORDS

Dawn Machell & Jane Horne

make believe ideas

Animals

dog

tortoise

goldfish

slug

whiskers

fur

cat

puppy

hamster

snail

kitten

octopus

fish

dolphin

mouse

penguin

jellyfish

fin

spout

shark

turtle

whale

sea lion

sea horse

beak

feathers

peacock

lion

zebra

wing

parrot

cub

wolf

monkey

rhinoceros

tiger

iguana

trunk

tusk

elephant

snake

crocodile

giraffe

hippopotamus

Let's go!

airplane

helicopter

car

bicycle

BIG TRUCK CO.

truck

tanker

limousine

motorcycle

garbage truck

school bus

STOP

train

underground train

hot-air balloon

rocket

space station

taxi

scooter

van

ladder

Whee-ooh!

siren

FIRE DEPT

fire truck

wheel

AMBULANCE

ambulance

POLICE

police car

digger

dump truck

boat

On the farm

rooster

gate

calf

tail

pig

hay

mane

piglet

horse

hoof

goose   gosling

farmer

chicken

chick

horse

plow

tractor

turkey

barn

cow

cat

fleece

lamb

sheep

horns

foal

goat

kid

sheepdog

pond

duck

duckling

In the forest

cloud

dragonfly

moth

butterfly

spider

web

bee

bear

caterpillar

trunk

grass

leaf

tent

acorn

fox

beetle

raccoon

campfire

rabbit

lizard

ladybug

worm

chick

nest

eagle

chipmunk

owl

branch

antlers

tree

woodpecker

twig

berries

moose

flower

bush

frog

rocks

log

pinecone

hedgehog

deer

badger

squirrel

toadstool

ant

television

rug

sofa

cushion

chair

vase

table

bubbles

toothbrush

faucet

toothpaste

sink

soap

SOAP

sponge

bathtub

towel

hairbrush

toilet roll

toilet

pan

oven

washing machine

refrigerator

grandma

grandpa

grandson

grandparents

granddaughter

adult

pregnant

aunt

uncle

friends

cousins

teenager

First Words Quiz

Can you remember what you have seen?

Practice first words by answering the questions, then ask an adult to make up some more!

Who has eight wiggly arms?

octopus

cat

snake

shark

What do you use to wash your clothes?

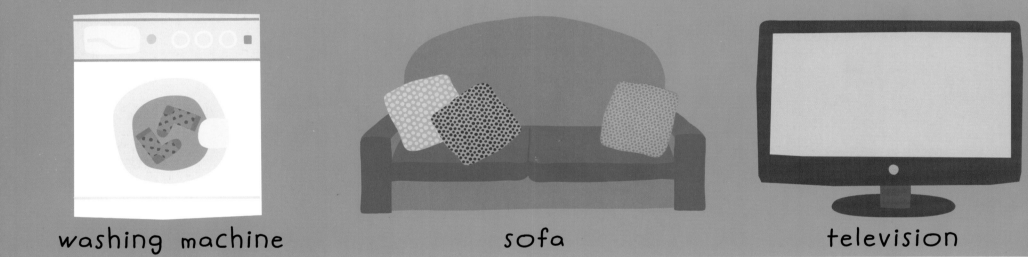

washing machine

sofa

television

Can you find the duck's baby?

duck

kitten

piglet

duckling

Point to the twins!

Which animal spins webs?

crocodile

spider

fox

Point to the train!

FIRE DEPT

pigtail

hair

forehead

eyebrow

nose

eyelash

ear

eye

cheek

mouth

freckle

chin

neck

lips

tongue

teeth

fingernail

toenail

finger

toe

muscle

thumb

heel

ankle

wrist

armpit

Getting dressed

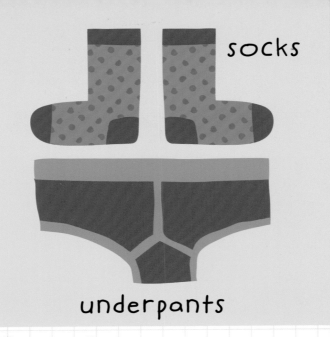
socks

underpants

vest

necklace

gloves

tights

mittens

clothes hanger

bow

cap

glasses

sweater

pants

sneakers

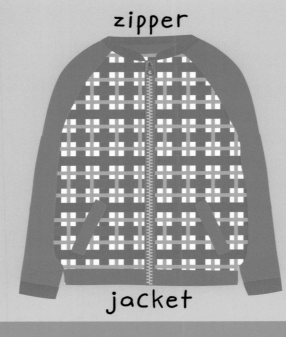
zipper

jacket

dress

shoelace

shoes

sun hat

sunglasses

belt

strap

shorts

sandals

T-shirt

coat

jeans

hood

tie

bag

shirt

sweatshirt

skirt

leggings

boots

hat

button

pajamas

scarf

pocket

cardigan

My toys

crown

knight

doll

building blocks

castle

teddy bear

train set

engine

track

Ee

Aa

Cc

cards

roller skates

skateboard

pirate

paddle and ball

drum

marbles

pirate ship

jigsaw puzzle

ball

kite

wand

fairy

dinosaur

YS

pen

pencil

paint   paintbrush

paper

STICKERS

stickers

crayons

monster

robot

dollhouse

clown

tambourine

xylophone

recorder

princess

tricycle

tea set

prince

tablet

Time to eat!

milk

yogurt

straw

WATER

water

juice

spoon

egg

toast

plate

fork

knife

cereal

cup and saucer

bread

broccoli

pumpki

cabbage

cheese

onion

potato

ham

peas

carrot

vegetables

corn

sandwich

fries

pizza

cake

rice

bowl

noodles

chopsticks

roast chicken

sausages

meat

cherry

cream

ice cream

peppers

lettuce

tomato

cucumber

avocado

mushrooms

olives

milk CHOCC

cookie

chocolate

grapes

pineapple

pear

orange

apple

banana

sauce

pasta

watermelon

fruit

strawberries

Opposites

fat

thin

tall

short

LUNCH

in

out

up

down

small

big

back

front

1 one

2 two

3 three

4 four

5 five

6 six

7 seven

8 eight

9 nine

10 ten

Numbers

Colors

red strawberry

yellow duckling

blue denim

green frog

pink dress

orange pumpkin

spotted ball

gray sea lion

gold crown

brown teddy bear

striped T-shirt

purple cloak

white mouse

black cat

silver armor

Shapes

square

circle

triangle

rectangle

oval

diamond

heart

star

First Words Quiz

Can you remember what you have seen?

Practice first words by answering the questions. then ask an adult to make up some more!

Which animal is green?

cat

frog

duckling

Who is sticking out their tongue?

Where does the knight live?

knight

house

cage

barn

castle

How many cupcakes can you count?

Point to the carrot!

Can you find the sleeping cat?

What do you wear at bedtime?

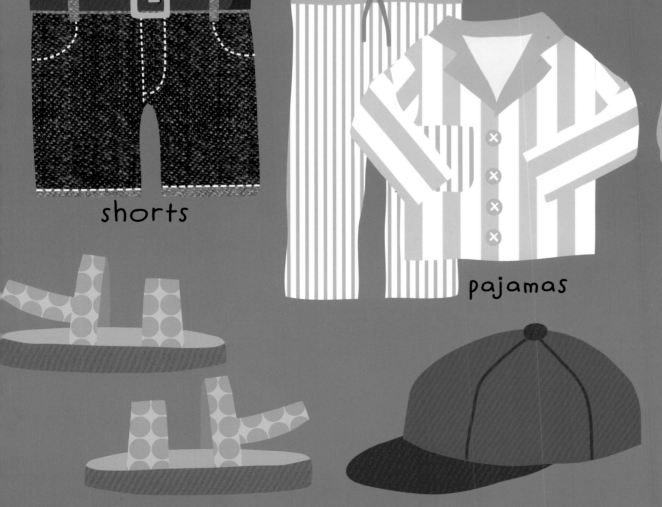

shorts

pajamas

sandals

cap